The Bean Straw
NON-FLYING OBJECTS

by

David Hammons

DMR Innovations, LLC

Oak Harbor, Washington, USA

ISBN: 978-0-6151-6349-9

"A merry heart doeth good like a medicine"
Proverbs 17:22

Anger Management

Snail discipline.

"I can't apologize enough for what happened. It was purely instinct ... I just reacted. If it's of any consolation to you, they were delicious!"

Tall Ned, local baby pusher scum.

Rex would quickly recover from his 400 puncture wounds, but it would be weeks before he could date again.

"Hey! ... Hey, Earl! ... I got another one!"

Bear vacations.

In the insect cave-exploring world, no cave was more challenging or awe-inspiring as "Big Ned's Inny."

8

Dracula finds that not only does their blood taste bad, bears are completely devoid of any sense of humor.

Wilbur knew that before this evening was over,
he was going to need the big fly swatter.

Needless to say, the horses were somewhat
concerned about Farmer John's new spurs.

"Why don't you stay outside with the other cattle? ...
And isn't that my shower cap?!"

On cold nights, buffalo were known to crawl into bed
with humans and steal the blanket.

Given the high-stakes poker and the volatility of the
players, cork horn safeties were required equipment.

"I told you not to jump on the bed!"

Although Rex was totally oblivious, his sudden run-ins
with the Dog Catcher could be blamed on the cat
and his new cell phone.

"Tried to throw the cat in the pool, didn't you?"

Hoping to be the first to introduce a new fashion to the disco scene, Ned's 'Towering Platform Shoes' were not well received.

Henry inadvertently mixes up his false teeth with his
novelty chattering teeth.

It was in desperate moments like these when Rex considered that whole "Man's Best Friend" business a bit overrated.

Nigel's short career as the local news channel's
on-the-spot weathervane.

"Sure - I'll flip a coin for the last one. Heads, I win.
Tails, I trample you into next week."

"See?! ... I hate it when that kid plays!"

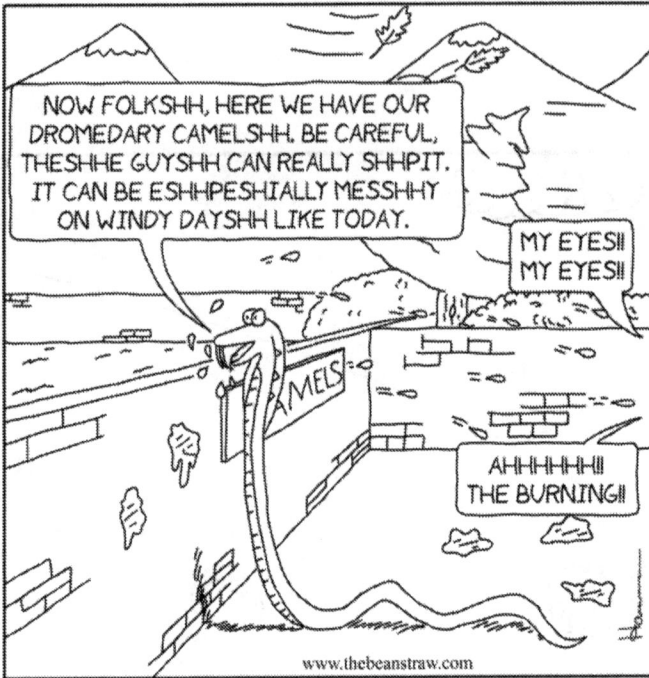

Spitting Cobras as zoo tour guides.

"Well, I'll be ... not even a whip ... just 17 cases of thumbscrews"

Dino dentures.

Clarence couldn't decide which was worse - buying his grandfather's 'special' underwear or taking them back because they were too small.

... AND BY THE WAY, I DON'T CARE FOR YOU COMING HERE EVERY STINKING DAY OF THE WEEK. SUNDAY IS THE ONLY DAY I GET A BREAK FROM YOU ... AND ANOTHER THING, YOU LOOK RIDICULOUS IN THOSE SHORT PANTS ... AND HAVE YOU EVER CONSIDERED PULLING THOSE SOCKS UP EVERY ONCE IN A WHILE!

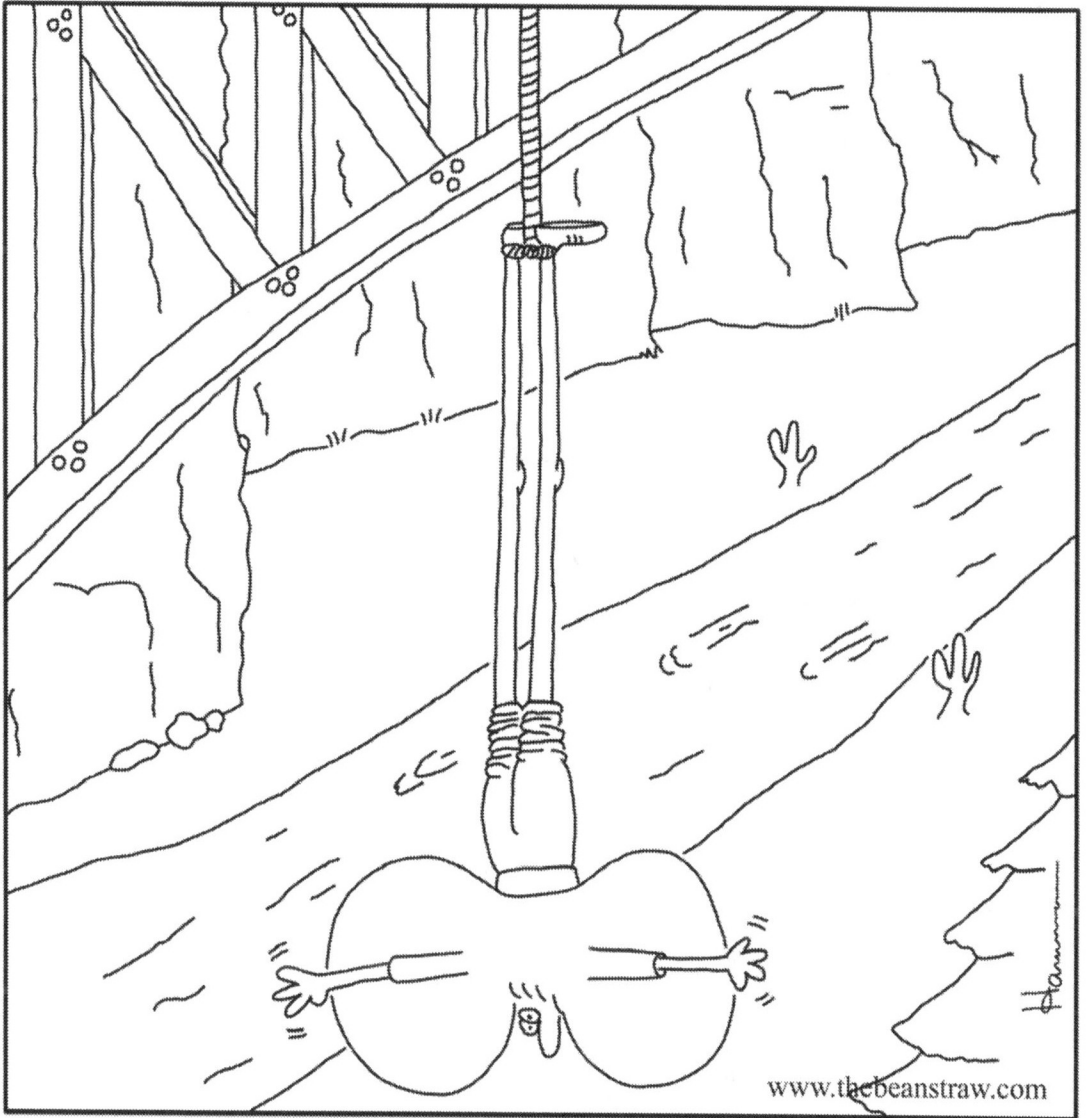

Early testing of potential bungee cords quickly
eliminated rope.

www.thebeanstraw.com

Dracula picks the wrong business to stalk ... and a
particularly ill-humored union night crew.

Young Webster forgot he had Nigel, 'The Mauler',
Bullinski in next period's rugby class.

When young Webster activated his home-made super electromagnet, he failed to consider his braces.

"Honestly, Honey, do you think this saddle makes my flanks look big?"

Fish vacations.

Although Ned was reasonably sure of his calculations, he couldn't help feeling something had gone terribly wrong.

It was on his third birthday when the Johnsons
discovered that Clarence had
'Flammable Breath' disorder.

When do-it-yourself home plumbing repairs
go wrong.

After Dr. Ned's mysterious disappearance, nothing more was heard of his "Clouds are Fluffy Balls of Cotton" theory.

"Well, of course I've got dog breath."

"Whoall ... Hang on a second, Honey. You may not want
to open that one. It's from the Dung Beetles"

"What?! So, the fancy new haircut wasn't enough, huh?! Now you want elbows!!"

"No, I don't know your name, Mister, but I'm
guessing it ain't Lefty."

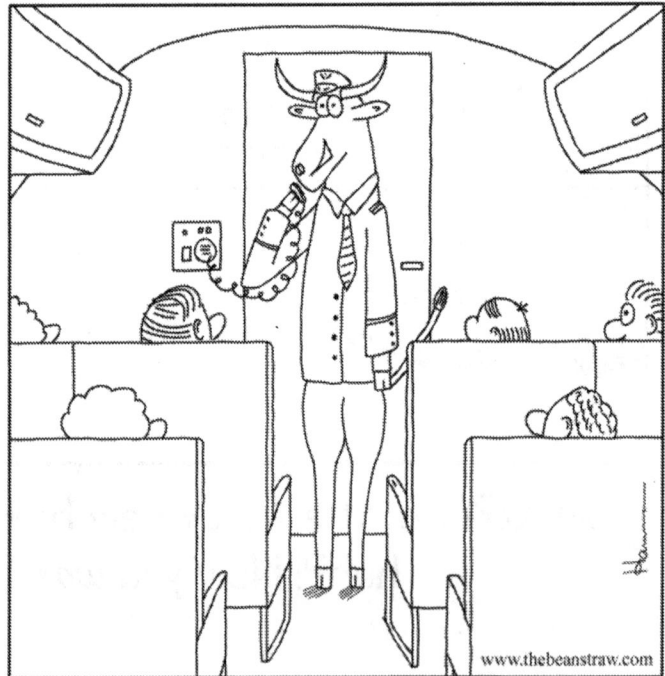

"Welcome aboard, ladies and gentlemen. I'll be your
captain for this evening's flight and ... yes ...
I'm a cow."

Ancient cliff dwellers experiment with elevator systems.

"Vacation paradise, my hoof! No air conditioning. Smelly old cattle truck. This trip couldn't get any worse. Well, now, what's the matter with you?!"

Darth Maul before he landed that Sith gig.

Death gets his robe back from the cleaners.

Domestic problems in the fly world.

A brilliant escape plan, blueprints of the factory,
rope, and a getaway car - all foiled by the cattle guard.

www.thebeanstraw.com

The Spring of 1911 saw the first attempt at a
bionic man.

Clarence attends a late night performance of
"Nedzini: Mindreader Extraordinaire."

"Hey guys, things are looking up! Now we just have to avoid sitting down until we're rescued."

Snakes and hot pavement.

"Oh yeah!?... Well, Godzilla is just a big, stupid lizard"

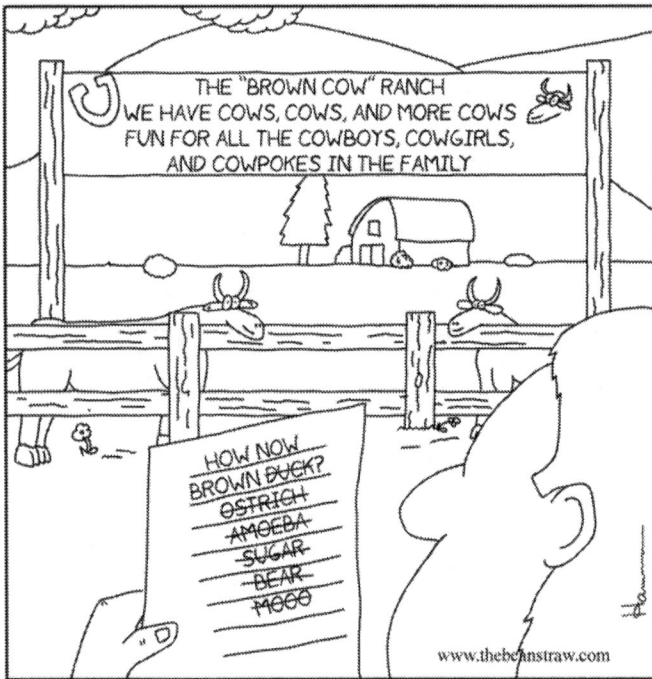

The constant mooing from the barnyard wasn't
helping Nigel's case of writer's block.

Hump building contests.

Giant squid families.

What really happened to Bo Peep's sheep.

"I'm sorry Mr. Johnson, but if you miss one more
payment, I'll have no choice but to eat you
and your family."

The villagers and lions had lived in secluded harmony until, one fateful day, Clarence licked one of them.

Dr. Nigel, psychiatrist, had seen many cases of Mad
Cow Disease, but this bovine was just plain crazy.

When love between co-workers and poor attempts
at humor collide.

How cows really sleep.

Using his speed and agility, Rex confirms that the light does go out and inadvertently activates his new refrigerator's auto-locking mechanism.

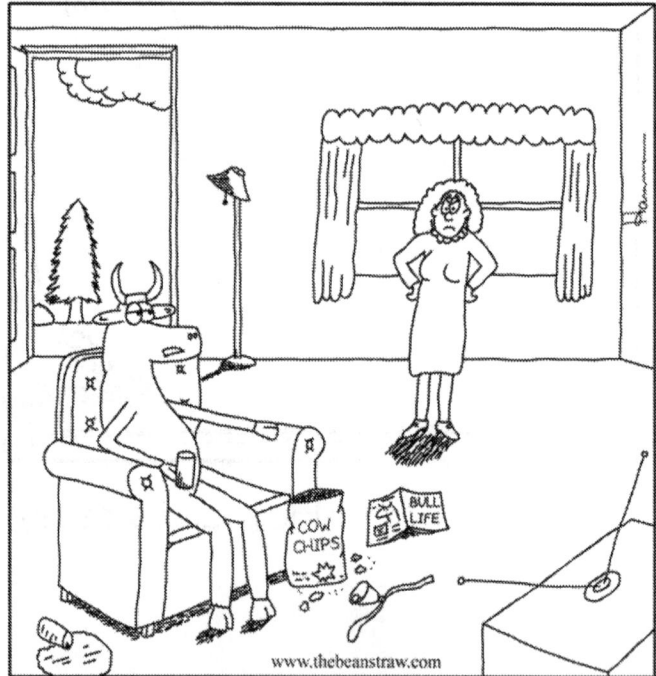

"Actually Dear, I was raised in a barn."

"Me and the boys hear that you don't let Rex sleep on the bed. Very disappointing, Mr. Johnson, VERY disappointing!"

"It was suicide, Mrs. Mallory. They found your husband
in a flashlight that had been left on all night."

In 1537, 'Ned the Menacing' was especially
intimidating with his spike helmet, big ax, platform
shoes, and his loyal sidekick some claimed was a dog.

Clarence: Nerd of the Jungle.

Nigel at the martial arts nunchicks competition.

Nigel's bat research team inadvertently disturbs a particularly nasty nest of "Tasmanian Sluggers."

Although Mrs. Johnson initially didn't like the children's new pet, she was able to find some practical uses for it.

Jedi mind tricks in the office.

"... uhhh ... Rex ... you sure these are the <u>flying</u> type?"

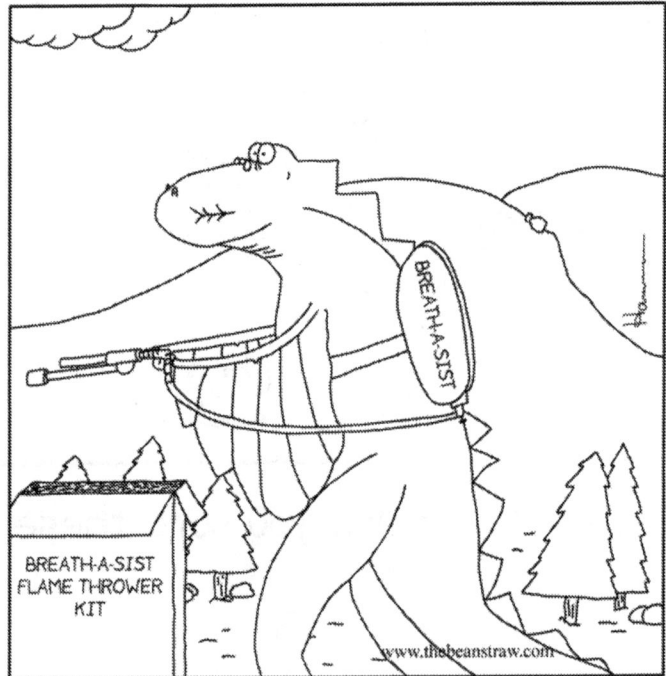

When older dragons need a little help.

Due to a sudden drop in business, Dr. Ned reconsiders his 'Reverse Psychology' advertising campaign.

"Hey, they got us packed in here like cattle! ... ha ... ha ... packed like ... hee ... hee ... get it? because we're ... ha ... ha ... sometimes I crack my own self up!"

"I just don't know how much more I can take, Doc. I feel like I'm going insane ... everyday, nothing but snow and penguins for miles and miles ..."

58

During their first performance, the orchestra discovers that all the rumors of their new conductor's previous career as a plumber were true.

Polar Bear dad's pet peeve.

Porcupine darts.

Prank duck calls.

Chiggy displayed his displeasure at being put out for
the night by giving the universally understood sign of
"The Claw."

Junior Possum's new toy startles the whole family.

www.thebeanstraw.com

When dogs ride in race cars.

Rock meetings.

After being told he is going to be a father, Nigel discovers a fact of seahorse life his parents never told him.

Shark traps.

Farmer Ned was going to put an end to his Roof
Clown problem once and for all.

Nigel unwittingly walks into the William Tell Archery Club's monthly meeting.

Snail vacations.

Since his declawing, Foo Foo was relentlessly taunted by the birds. Then he discovered the sportsman's shop down the street.

Flipping through the dictionary one night, Clarence discovers what cud really is.

With a desperate criminal on the loose and no Blood-hounds available, the State Police turn to the less popular Photohound for help.

"Sunburn? Hah! ... I got stuck in a nuclear reactor for three hours. Now, that was a sunburn. But after a couple of days and a little peeling, I was good as new."

72

Unlike Jane Goodall and the chimpanzees, Ned's attempts to live with Western Diamondbacks were less successful.

"If I positioned the magnifying glass correctly, we're in for some serious tanning."

www.thebeanstraw.com

www.thebeanstraw.com

Ned thought he could save money by enrolling in a
telekinetics correspondence course.

The new super heroes: Bug Eye, Radar, and The Schnoz.

Snake boxing.

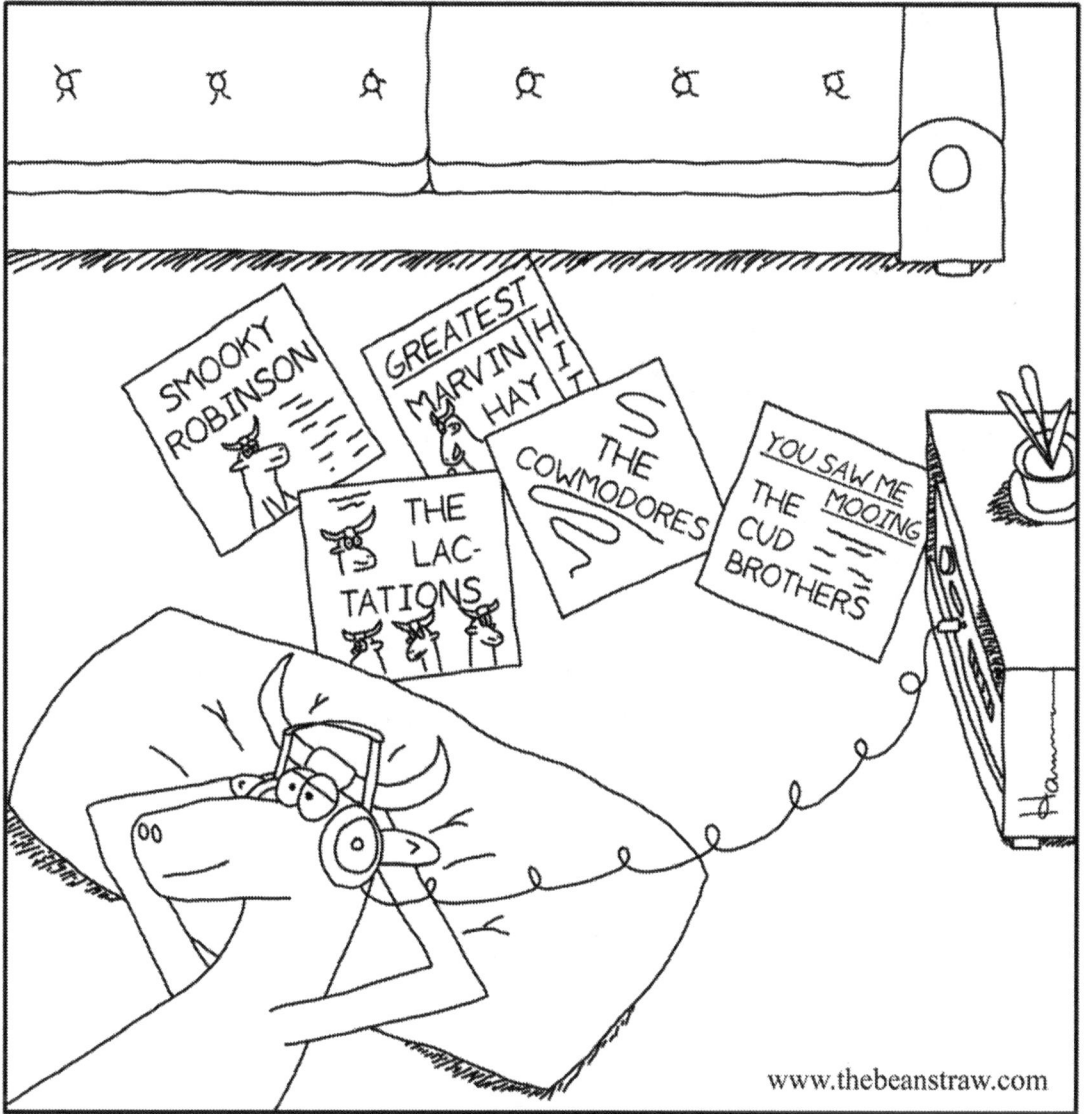

Clarence liked lying back, relaxing, and listening to
a little classic Moo-town.

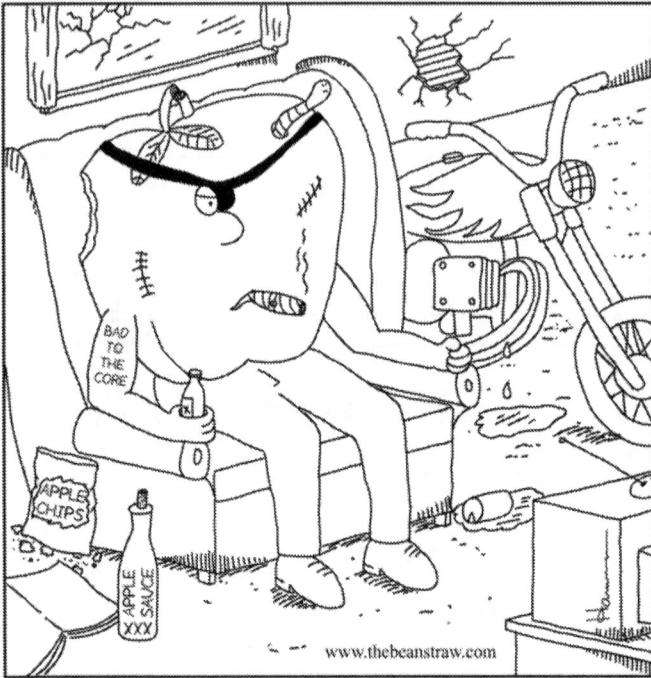

No one knows exactly how or when, but Johnny
was one apple that had just plain gone bad.

It is believed that the Persian cat developed its
distinctive flat face during the medieval period.

"You're going to pay the boss back, see ... or you're going to have a little talk with my friend Sammy 'The Slapper' here."

Farmer John found it hard to take the cows' threat
to unionize seriously.

"Whoa ... Hank ... When's the last time you've been to
the watering hole?"

www.thebeanstraw.com

81

The sure signs of money and prestige in the farming
world are slicked-back hair, bow tie, and a
Stretch Cow parked in front of the barn.

After living with the wild dogs of Idaho for six years,
Ned makes the first communicative contact.

DO NOT THROW OBJECTS FROM BRIDGE

www.thebeanstraw.com

"For crying out loud, Edna, put this back on the road! ... it's still alive!"

Tempers flare over the design of the first airplane and the word 'dork' is introduced to the English language.

"Well, that's the last of the food supplies!"

Mummy laundry days.

When cows help around the farm.

www.ingramcontent.com/pod-product-compliance
Lightning Source LLC
Chambersburg PA
CBHW062107090426
42741CB00015B/3356